ORGANIZING YOUR MOVE:
Moving Checklists, Worksheets and Timeline

Jenny Cogan

TABLE OF CONTENTS

INTRODUCTION i

ORGANIZE YOUR MOVE
CHAPTER 1: GETTING STARTED 1

CHAPTER 2: SORTING AND DECLUTTERING 3
What to keep 3
Staying organized while sorting 4

CHAPTER 3: PACKING SUPPLIES & OVERVIEW 5
List of Packing Supplies 6
Decide on method for organizing your boxes 8
Colors (labels or tape) for each room 8
What not to pack/Hazardous Materials 9

CHAPTER 4: PACKING YOUR BOXES 12
How to Pack 12
Kitchen & Dining 14
Bedrooms & Bathrooms 14
Family Room, Living Room, and Office 15
Garage, Yard, and Attic 15

MOVING
CHAPTER 5: DECIDE ON YOUR METHOD OF MOVING 17
Methods of moving 17
Start talking to movers & questions to ask 18

CHAPTER 6: MOVING BUDGET AND QUOTES 22
Ways to save money on your budget 23
Formulate your budget 24

CHAPTER 7: LEAVING YOUR CURRENT HOME, AND WHAT ABOUT
A NEW HOME? 28
Cleaning your home, leaving key items behind for new resident, changing the locks

CHAPTER 8: PREPARING FOR YOUR FIRST NIGHT IN YOUR NEW HOME ... 29
First Night Essentials Checklist 29

CHAPTER 9: CHANGE OF ADDRESS 31

CHAPTER 10: MOVING TIMELINE 34

COMMAND CENTER 48
Itinerary Overview 49
Contacts 50
Inventory Sheets of personal belongings 59
Grid Paper for notes, laying out of furniture in new home, etc 93

INTRODUCTION

Moving... a magical word for some, full of excitement, hope, and change. For others, the word can generate feelings of stress or overwhelm. What do I do? Where do I start? When do I start? How do I do it? The questions can be endless. But it doesn't have to be overwhelming, you may just need a little bit of help getting started on the right foot and staying organized.

I have simplified the process for you in this book with various checklists, worksheets and even a timeline. On page 34 you will find the Moving Timeline which is not only a big overview of the entire moving process with things broken down into steps, it is also a convenient checklist for you to mark off each task as completed. I have provided blank lines on each form so that you can personalize them with specifics that pertain to your unique moving situation.

These checklists, worksheets, and moving timeline were a tremendous help for me with my own move. I was excited and hopeful but soon realized that I needed to be organized if I wanted to keep those positive feelings. I am sharing what worked for me. I am encouraging you to take this book and tweak it and make it your own, this is your moving journey so make this book work for you. Write in it, take notes, add stickies to the pages you use most often, and let it assist you on your own move.

Happy moving!

ORGANIZE YOUR MOVE

CHAPTER 1: GETTING STARTED

Organization, the foundation to a successful move and key to minimizing stress. Knowing the Big Picture of What, When, Why, etc and breaking it down into manageable steps is key for a smooth move, which makes the whole process more enjoyable.

First thing I would recommend is that you familiarize yourself with this whole book, look at the topics covered and check out the various forms and checklists. Know what is in it and where to find it.

Second, I encourage you to set up a system to help keep your receipts, quotes, medical records, school records, etc organized. Use a large envelope, folder, pocket, or my personal favorite, binder with tabs, as a place to keep track of these papers. If you are going to be reimbursed for this move or claim it on your taxes, this will be very important. Also create a folder on the desktop of your computer for saving all digital files and documents pertinent for your move. You should also print out these digital files and documents and add them to your binder behind the appropriate tab as a backup.

TIP: Do you have children? Include them in on the process as soon as possible so they can have this time to adjust to the idea of moving and participate based on their age and level of understanding. Set a tone for your move... schedule in extra play dates with their best friends, visit your favorite local spots, and even plan a Going Away Party. Organize and schedule these activities in just as you would anything else. And don't forget to tell your children about the great new spots that you can't wait to explore with them once you move. New parks? Zoos? Museums? Help them get excited about the adventure ahead.

PEOPLE TO SEE AND THINGS TO DO BEFORE WE MOVE:

Ask everyone in your family if there is anyone that they would like to see or anything that they would like to do before the move and make notes of all of the ideas here.

_____   _____

_____   _____

_____   _____

_____   _____

_____

THINGS TO SEE AND DO AFTER WE SETTLE INTO OUR NEW HOME:

Create a list of the new things to see and do that will excite your children about the move.

_____ _____

_____ _____

_____ _____

_____ _____

_____ _____

NOTES:

_____

_____

_____

_____

_____

CHAPTER 2: SORTING AND DECLUTTERING

Typically it is recommended to start preparing for a move at least 6-8 weeks before the actual move date but I would highly recommend that you start this process as soon as you decide that you will move, even if it is 6-12 months before the move. This allows you more time to do what needs to be done, like sorting through all of your belongings without a tight time frame looming ahead. Sorting can often slow people down so make sure that you give yourself enough time to complete the process without being overwhelmed or stressed. Also, by starting the sorting and decluttering process early enough, you will have the time to sell the items that you want to sell, make your donations, and even begin packing out-of-season items at a more relaxed pace.

Additional benefits to sorting and decluttering:

1. Why pay to move things that you actually don't want or need? This is one way to reduce total moving expenses by not having to pay for more space on a truck, needing fewer packing supplies, etc. It will also make your moving quote more accurate if you complete this before having a full-service mover come out to your home to give you a quote.

2. Sorting and decluttering as you are packing can slow you down. By doing it beforehand you can just focus on sorting and decluttering (and then selling and donating) and when it comes time for packing you can focus just on packing.

3. You might be able to sell some of those unneeded items and apply that money towards your move.

4. You will have less to unpack at your new home and can get settled in more quickly.

By the time you are 1-2 months away from the actual move date you will have already completed a huge part of the moving process which reduces "last minute" stress.

WHAT TO KEEP

Going through your items and deciding what to keep and what to get rid of can be a very personal process. You don't want to have any regrets by getting rid of something that you later realize you should have kept, so here are some questions you could ask yourself to help you decide what to keep and what to get rid of:

Do I love this?

Does it make me smile every time I see it, wear it, use it, etc?

Do I wear this?

Do I use this? Even if not regularly, maybe I only use it to make my Famous Thanksgiving dinner, but is it useful to me?

Is this item expired?

Is this item in good condition? Is it broken? Need to be repaired? Can it be repaired?

Does this item have sentimental value to me?

If you are looking for a method or process to assist you with decluttering, there are different methods and ideas out there. One is the KonMari method created by Marie Kondo, the author of the book "The Life-Changing Magic of Tidying Up: The Japanese Method of Decluttering and Organizing." Her focus is on keeping what "sparks joy" or what you love, which resonates with many people. What could be better than being in your new home surrounded by things that you absolutely love? She has a specific order that she recommends one use when sorting through their belongings, starting with categories that are typically easier for most people, such as clothing, progressing until you arrive at the hardest categories, such as sentimentals. Please check out her book for more information. Some people love a focus on minimalism and try to keep their belongings to a very basic level. Some people just get rid of things they don't really use and that is simple enough for them. Take what resonates with you and do your own thing. This is your process, your move.

STAYING ORGANIZED WHILE SORTING

The 4 box method is a very popular way to organize items as you sort through your belongings. The boxes can be easily labeled into categories such as "Keep," "Trash," "Sell," and "Donate." As you sort, immediately place the item into the appropriate box. If you do not have 4 spare boxes you can use trash bags. Once a box is filled you can take the appropriate action: pack, toss, sell, or donate.

TIP: Depending on the type of items in your "Sell" box, you may decide to list and sell each item immediately or you may choose to wait until you have collected enough items to hold a yard sale. Some items may sell for a higher price on eBay vs a yard sale but then you will have to mail the item, so you may want to do your research and see what works best for you.

NOTES:

_____

_____

_____

_____

_____

CHAPTER 3: PACKING SUPPLIES & OVERVIEW

STOP. Before packing, have you sorted and decluttered your belongings? Put aside the items that you will not be taking with you? Have you donated them or begun the process of selling them? If not, go back to Chapter 2 and begin that process. OK, you did declutter? Now that you are ready to pack, let's go on to the next step.

PACKING SUPPLIES

Now that you've sorted and decluttered, you will be able to look at your belongings and get a more accurate idea of what packing supplies will be needed. Have a lot of books? You will need plenty of small boxes as larger boxes easily become too heavy. Have bulky but light items that require large boxes? Lampshades can fit into this category. How about a lot of glass or breakables? Will you be needing a lot of bubble wrap? Will you be moving large appliances or large pieces of furniture such as a cabinet or buffet? How many furniture pads would you then need? Moving a lot of artwork or mirrors? A flat screen TV? It is good to begin thinking about your specific needs and develop a general plan before you begin gathering packing supplies.

For moving boxes, you can often pick up free boxes at grocery stores or liquor stores. Call ahead and talk to the managers first, find out if they have boxes and what would be the best time for you to come and pick them up. Make sure that the boxes are clean, sturdy and in great condition with no water damage. Also, you can often find free boxes offered by people who have recently moved. Tell your family and friends that you are looking for boxes so that they can help you.

If you don't have time to chase down free boxes, you can often purchase basic boxes in various sizes at hardware stores and moving truck rental companies. As I was alluding to earlier, you can also purchase specialty boxes for flat panel TVs, pictures and mirrors, boxes with dividers for glasses, wardrobe boxes for clothing, and much more at moving truck rental companies. Also, you can order packing supplies online and they can arrive at your home in a matter of days, so explore your options.

Moving truck rental companies can also carry items that you can rent, such as hand trucks and furniture pads.

TIP: you can save money on packing supplies by using clothes, socks, towels, sheets and blankets to wrap some of your personal belongings, cushion them, or to even finish filling up a box so the box is full with no wasted space. This would also be a great time to save any air pillows, packing paper, or boxes that you receive in the mail from online orders. I stuff air pillows and packing paper into a box or large trash bag and save them for later, this not only keeps it all neatly contained but also clean and dust-free.

LIST OF PACKING SUPPLIES:

☐ rolls of quality packing tape

☐ tape dispensers (the dispenser "gun" where there is a long handle is the most convenient)

☐ bubble wrap

☐ packing paper to wrap your items and to finish filling up a box (newspaper can also be used to fill up a box, just make sure that all of your items are pre-wrapped in packing paper so that ink will not transfer onto them)

☐ foam pouches made for glass plates and glasses

☐ stretch plastic wrap, can be used in different ways, such as wrapping furniture to keep drawers or doors closed, or can be used to secure a furniture pad over furniture or an appliance

☐ furniture pads

☐ mattress bags (keeps your mattresses clean)

☐ tool kit for disassembling furniture (screwdrivers, wrenches, sockets, hammer, etc. If using electric, make sure batteries are fully charged)

☐ zipper food storage bags are good for keeping screws, washers, etc from furniture together (label bags with a permanent marker so that you know what piece of furniture it belongs to)

☐ permanent markers for labeling storage bags and boxes

☐ pen or pencil to update the forms in this book

☐ labels

☐ box cutter or utility knife

☐ scissors

☐ boxes, miscellaneous sizes depending on your needs

☐ smaller boxes are good for heavy items such as books, 12"x12" is good, be sure to not over pack

☐ medium boxes are good for toys, kitchen items, etc

☐ large boxes are good for lightweight items such as lamp shades, comforters, etc

☐ box for flat screen TV

☐ boxes with dividers are sold at moving truck rental facilities, great for glasses

☐ mirror/picture frame boxes

☐ wardrobe boxes for coats, jackets, suits, etc.

☐ trash bags (good for stuffed animals, comforters, pillows, etc to keep them clean)

☐ bungee cords or rope to keep items in the moving truck from shifting

☐ back brace

☐ gloves

☐ forearm strap (straps that two people use together to help them lift heavy objects)

☐ hand truck

☐ a padlock to secure the back of the moving truck

☐ _____

☐ _____

☐ _____

☐ _____

DECIDE ON METHOD FOR ORGANIZING YOUR BOXES

Now that you have decluttered and gathered packing supplies, it is time to decide on a method for organizing your boxes. It makes it so much easier to unpack your boxes in an organized, systematic way if from the beginning they are packed and labeled in an organized, systematic way, which is per the room for which the items in the box belong.

Three common ways to do this:

1. Grab a large marker and label each box with the name of the room that the contents belong in

2. Purchase tape in various colors and assign a color for each room, as your boxes are filled you place a strip of the tape, maybe 3 or 4 inches long, on the box. As your boxes are unloaded from the truck you can easily sort them at a glance by color and put them in the correct room for easier unpacking (example: kitchen = orange, living room = blue, etc).

3. You can purchase pre-printed, color-coordinated room label sets (labels for the most common rooms such as kitchen, living room, bedroom, etc) or create them yourself and print them out on label paper. Make sure that you have plenty of ink to finish the job.

COLORS FOR EACH ROOM

Kitchen: _____

Family Room: _____

Living Room: _____

Dining Room _____

Master Bedroom _____

Bedroom 2: _____

Bedroom 3: _____

Bedroom 4: _____

Master Bathroom: _____

2nd Bathroom: _____

3rd Bathroom: _____

Office: _____

Basement: _____

Laundry room: _____

Utility/Garage: _____

Storage: _____

TIP: tape a piece of paper with the correct color on the doorway of each room in your new home to help everyone remember what color goes with what room or have a master list posted upon entering your new home.

After determining how you will organize your boxes by room, the next most important thing is numbering each box for each room in sequential order. This is important for two reasons, that way you can verify that each box arrived in your new home and when it comes to unpacking, you can, with the help of your Inventory sheets, go directly to the box that contains the items that you currently need to unpack first. Number each box with a marker or you can use those little circular dot stickers (also can be color coordinated if desired). Start with number 1 and continue numbering your boxes in sequential order until everything for that room and color are boxed.

Make sure you write down the contents in each box on the Inventory spreadsheets at the back of this book on page 59 before you tape your box shut. After all of the sorting and decluttering that you've been doing, this is the perfect time to take inventory of what you have left. This can be helpful for insurance purposes and if you need to file a claim due to a missing box or damage to some of your belongings if you hire a moving service. As each box comes off of the truck, mark it as Arrived. Make note if the box and its contents have not arrived in good condition, you may need to file a claim.

TIP: take a photo of the condition of items that you are particularly concerned about before packing

Also, having an inventory of each numbered box is very helpful when unpacking as you can focus on unpacking the most needed items first. And if you need to find something specific like your cookie sheet, look on the Inventory sheet for Kitchen and find the box # that it was packed in. You can now go straight to it.

No matter which of the three ways you decide to organize your boxes by room (marker, colorful tape or color-coordinated room labels), make sure that you number each box and note the contents on the inventory spreadsheets. It will enable you to unpack your boxes in an orderly way by focusing on the contents most needed first.

TIP: For my move, I kept separate inventory sheets for each room of the house so that all of my kitchen boxes and their contents are together on a spreadsheet labeled Kitchen, all of my living room boxes and their contents are together on a spreadsheet labeled Living Room, etc.

WHAT NOT TO PACK

PLANTS:

While plants may not be an automatic "Do Not Pack" and can often be packed and moved, there are two issues that need to be taken into consideration if you are moving across state lines and across long distances:

Does your new home state allow you to bring in plants across state lines? Due to gypsy moth infestations and other issues some states strictly regulate bringing in possibly contaminated plants.

How long is the drive and will your plants survive the drive without sun or water? Also the temperature inside the moving truck, hot in summer/cold in winter can kill many plants.

If you are moving across state lines I encourage you to research the laws of your new home state to see if they have any laws or regulations that you must follow in order to bring your plans in legally and avoid any problems or fines.

HAZARDOUS MATERIALS THAT SHOULD NOT BE PACKED:

This list contains common flammable, combustible, and explosive items that movers will not move. Please check with your moving company to get their complete, up-to-date list.

- ☐ Acids/Ammonia
- ☐ Aerosol cans (deodorant, hair spray)
- ☐ Antifreeze
- ☐ Batteries/Car Batteries
- ☐ Black powder, smokeless powder
- ☐ Candles
- ☐ Charcoal
- ☐ Chemistry sets
- ☐ Cleaning supplies/bleach
- ☐ Compressed gases
- ☐ Dangerous or unidentified liquids
- ☐ Disinfectants
- ☐ Dyes
- ☐ Fire extinguishers
- ☐ Firearms and ammunition
- ☐ Fireworks
- ☐ Fluid cleaners

- ☐ Gasoline/Kerosene or other petroleum products
- ☐ Igniters or primers
- ☐ Lamp oil
- ☐ Lighter fluid
- ☐ Liquor (alcoholic beverages)
- ☐ Matches
- ☐ Motor oil
- ☐ Nail polish and nail polish remover
- ☐ Paint, paint thinners, and other paint-related materials
- ☐ Pesticides/Fertilizer/Weed killers/Poisons
- ☐ Pool chemicals
- ☐ Propane, propane tanks
- ☐ Propellers (propellants?)
- ☐ Rubbing alcohol
- ☐ Scuba diving tanks
- ☐ Signal flares
- ☐ Sterno fuel
- ☐ Yard equipment containing fuel

NOTES:

_____

_____

_____

_____

_____

CHAPTER 4: PACKING YOUR BOXES

You have your packing supplies and have decided on how you are going to keep track of your boxes, now it is time to pack! I enjoyed sorting and decluttering and I enjoyed gathering packing supplies, and I really enjoyed packing! I don't know, something about it, I think it just made the whole move that much more real to me.

It is always advisable to start packing those items that you do not expect to use until after you have moved into your new home... seasonal decor, items in the attic or garage, books, etc.
Make sure that you number and label each box and fill out your Inventory spreadsheet as you pack each box, double-check that the number, label, and spreadsheet are accurate and match.
Start by assembling a box, securing the bottom flaps with tape. Also run a strip of tape perpendicular to the seam of the bottom flaps of the box for extra security, I also like to run a strip of tape on the inside of boxes, especially if they will be holding heavy items such as books. If using boxes found at a grocery store or elsewhere, check the tape, secure the box with additional tape if necessary.

HOW TO PACK

Put crumpled packing paper on the bottom of boxes before filling. Wrap items in paper or bubble wrap and place in box, fill empty spaces in the corners. sides, and on top of items with more crumpled paper, making sure that each box is filled completely. This will prevent items from shifting and the box from being crushed due to empty gaps within the box when other boxes are stacked on top of it.

If packing different types of items in a box, put the heavier items on the bottom and the lighter, more delicate items on the top.

Also, pack so that weight of the items in each box is evenly distributed, if the weight in the box is not evenly distributed this lopsidedness could cause a box to fall or roll easily and items could break.

Remember to pack heavy items like books in smaller boxes like 12" x 12."

The boxes with cell kits sold at moving truck rental stores for glasses will work for so many other uses: glass jars from your pantry, candle sticks, knickknacks, and much more.

Light items such as comforters, blankets, and pillows can be packed in trash bags, this will not only keep them clean but you can then use the bags to stuff between boxes and furniture in the back of the moving truck to help keep items from shifting during the move. Once at your new home you can reuse these bags for trash.

Disassemble furniture if possible, it will arrive at your destination in better condition and items will pack better in the back of the truck. Put all screws, bolts, etc for each piece of furniture in a zippered sandwich bag, label bag with a permanent marker, and tape bag on the underside of furniture so they are kept together (or you can keep all zippered and labeled bags of furniture screws and bolts together in a basket with your tools). Wrap furniture in furniture pads and then secure pads with plastic wrap. Not only will the plastic wrap secure the furniture pad to the furniture, but plastic wrap can damage some finishes so it is best to use a furniture pad beneath plastic wrap.

If you still have the original boxes for electronics and appliances, use them.

Delicate items or sensitive electronics should be wrapped in paper, cushioned and boxed, and this box should be placed in a larger box, cushioned well.

Remove lamp shades and bulbs before packing.

Now is a good time to have any area rugs cleaned before packing.

Mark boxes carrying glass or delicate items "Fragile." You can also purchase stickers that say "Fragile" on them. Putting stickers on fragile boxes was a fun thing for my children to do to participate in the moving process.

IMPORTANT: All valuables such as jewelry, important documents such as birth certificates, passports, financial records, etc should be moved by you personally and not be placed the back of a truck.

KITCHEN & DINING

I am a fan of the boxes for dishes and glasses that you can purchase at moving truck rental stores. Not only are the boxes very sturdy, they come with dividers that separate out your items and include foam pockets that you can put each item in for extra cushion.

If you choose to not use the boxes for glasses, please remember to wrap each glass generously with paper or bubble wrap and to not lay glasses on their sides when packing, that increases the chance of breakage.

As stated above, use original boxes for appliances (toaster, coffee pot, etc) if you still have them. Otherwise, wrap and cushion appliances very well.

Wrap appliances and furniture with furniture pads and then plastic wrap.

When packing knives, take extra precaution to wrap them well. Have a stack of wrapping paper laid out on the table surface, place a knife near a corner and pull up a few pieces of paper and wrap over the knife, rolling the knife a couple of times, then place a second knife next to the first one with the blade going in the opposite direction, rolling that stack a few times, then repeat the process with a 3rd and then a 4th knife, if the paper allows. Tape the package closed and label it "Knives" so when it comes time to unpack the person knows to be careful. Repeat this process until all of your sharp knives are well wrapped.

When packing pots and pans, put two pieces of packing paper in the bottom of the largest pot, place the next smaller pot inside of it, add two pieces of paper into that pot, place the next small pot into that pot, and continue until completed. Wrap entire bundle of pots with more packing paper, tape, and place into box, completely filling out box with packing paper.

BEDROOMS & BATHROOMS

Stretch plastic wrap can be used on dressers to keep the drawers closed in transit. If the dresser is not too heavy, you can even leave the clothing in the drawers before plastic wrapping. If the clothes make it too heavy just remove them and pack them in suitcases or boxes or even trash bags (clothes in trash bags can be used to cushion furniture in the back of the moving truck). Plastic wrap can damage some surfaces so it is better to wrap the furniture piece first with a furniture pad before using the plastic wrap as a precaution.

Wardrobe boxes are great for suits, coats, etc. Some people like to pack their shoes in the available space in the bottom of the boxes.

Another method for packing hanging clothing is to leave clothes on the hanger, open up a trash bag and fit it over the bottom of the bunch of clothes and carefully pull the bag up to the level of the hanger with all of the clothes neatly inside of the bag, then tie the trash bag around the neck of the hangers. Not only will your clothes remain clean but when you unpack them you just remove the bag and presto hang them up and you are done. The trash bag can be then be reused.

Make sure that you do not pack medications that you will need while you move and settle into your new home.

Make sure that you do not pack personal care items that you will need while you move and settle into your new home, such as toothpaste, shampoo, etc.

For the personal care items that you will be packing, take the lid off of the bottles and put a small piece of plastic wrap over the top and replace the lid. This will prevent leaks.

Do not pack baby items that you will need immediately and make sure that you have favorite toys, stuffed animals, coloring books, etc, left out for your children so that they will have something to play with during the moving and settling in process.

Use mattress bags to keep mattresses and box springs clean when they are in the back of the moving truck. My daughter had a very large stuffed bear that she adored, a mattress bag was perfect for keeping it clean in the back of the moving truck.

FAMILY ROOM, LIVING ROOM, & OFFICE

As stated above, use original boxes for electronics (DVD player, computer, etc) if you still have them. Otherwise, wrap and cushion electronics very well.

Before packing computer equipment, make copies of your files on a thumb drive or store online through a site like Dropbox.

Take photos of how electronics are wired together and set up before disassembling. If needed, label cords and connections on the device (use tape and write notes on the end of the wire and to where it connects or colored stickers would also be useful, different colors to match up different wires to different connection points).

Make sure electronics are cooled to room temperature before packing.

Games, DVDs and CDs can get heavy quickly so pack in smaller boxes.

GARAGE, YARD, AND ATTIC

Drain the oil and gas from lawn equipment (mower, edger, chain saw, etc). Review Hazardous Materials list of things not to pack on page 9-10.

Use original boxes to pack electric tools if you still have them. Remove battery beforehand.

Plastic wrap can be used to keep tool boxes closed.

Wrap the sharp ends of pick axes, saws, shears, shovels, hoes, etc. with bubble wrap or blankets or towels. Items with long handles can be bundled together and the bottom ends can be wrapped with a blanket or towel.

Wash patio furniture, cushions, umbrellas, bird baths/houses/feeders, garden decor, pots and planters, etc and let them dry thoroughly. Furniture may need to be disassembled. If there are glass tabletops use extra caution when packing these to prevent breakage. Trash bags can be used to cover and protect cushions and umbrellas. Carefully bubble wrap and pack bird baths/houses, feeders, garden decor, pots and planters as needed.

Check with your moving company, propane tanks, even if empty, may not be allowed on the truck.

NOTES:

_____

_____

_____

_____

_____

MOVING

CHAPTER 5: DECIDE ON YOUR METHOD OF MOVING

What are the main methods of moving? What do they involve? What are the main differences? How do I decide which one is right for me? How do they affect my budget? Let's take a look.

METHODS OF MOVING

Let us briefly discuss the four main methods of moving as they will have a huge impact on your involvement in the moving process and ultimately budget. At the end of this chapter I have included a list of questions to ask various moving companies so that you can better understand their services and can therefore make an accurate comparison based on those services and prices.

Truck rental: you pack, load, drive, unload, unpack, and set up furniture. The most cost effective but also the most time and labor intensive. You provide packing supplies. **Pros**: most budget friendly moving option, your items arrive at your destination when you do, you get to drive a truck. **Cons**: you need to pack your items well to prevent breakage in transit; don't forget to add gas for the truck rental and your personal travel expenses into your budget, you may need to hire labor to help you move your heavy items (or pay friends with pizza), you get to drive a truck.

Freight company/pay-by-the-foot: you pack and load your belongings into the back of a truck and you pay based on the square footage of space used. Company drives truck, you unload, unpack, set up furniture. You provide packing supplies. **Pros**: you only pay for the amount of space you use, they drive which means you can fly to your destination or drive and sightsee along the way. **Cons**: you need to pack your items well to prevent breakage in transit; don't forget to add your personal travel expenses into your budget, you may need to hire labor to help you move your heavy items (or pay friends with pizza).

Storage containers: company delivers storage containers to your driveway, you pack, load, they pick up, drive, and will store them for you if needed. You unload, unpack, set up your furniture. You provide packing supplies. **Pros**: they drive which means you can fly to your destination or drive and sightsee along the way, they will put the storage containers in their storage facility and keep them (for a fee) until you are ready for them to be delivered. **Cons**: you need to pack your items well to prevent breakage, delivery is not fast if you need your items right away so plan ahead; don't forget to add your personal travel expenses into your budget, and you may need to hire labor to help you move your heavy items (or pay friends with pizza).

Full-service movers: they pack, load, deliver, unload, unpack, and set up your furniture for you. Packing supplies are provided. Much is managed for you which also makes it the most expensive method of moving. They will need to come to your house and see what they will be moving in order to give you an accurate quote. **Pros**: they do all of the labor which is important if you are elderly or are dealing with health issues, have to work, or maybe you have valuable antiques that you want to have the white glove treatment; you can file a claim if items break in transit; you can fly to your destination or drive and sightsee along the way. **Cons**: don't forget to add your personal travel expenses into your budget; is the most expensive moving option.

START TALKING TO MOVERS

Now that you are familiar with the main ways to move and what will be required from you physically, time wise, etc, some methods will immediately be acceptable to you and some will not. You can begin talking to movers, get price quotes and move forward with the process when you are ready.

But if you are still unsure and want to do a little more research first, here are a few things that you can do to gather a bit more information to be better prepared before calling.

Several moving companies have online calculators to give you a rough estimate of how much a move will cost based on how many bedrooms of furniture you have to move and the distance. Some calculators have you estimate the number of boxes and furniture pieces that you want to move and it provides you with an estimate. Some truck rental company websites have simple calculators where you enter in the date of your move and the zip codes of your current location and destination, how many bedrooms are in your current home, and it will give you quotes with prices noted for each size of truck available, you can also get a quote for the price for towing equipment if you need to tow a vehicle. These can be helpful for you in the beginning just to get a general idea of how much each moving method differs in price and services, but in the end you really need to contact each moving company and start talking to them, ask questions, and get more detailed information that pertains to you and your personal situation. Full-service movers have to come to your home and see what they will be moving in order to give you an accurate quote.

Note if there are any special circumstances with your home's location, are the streets narrow, is your driveway on a steep hill, is there enough room for a truck to turn around or can it just pass through, will you need to get a permit for a truck or storage container to be parked? Find out what each company needs in regards to space to park the truck or storage container.

This chapter overlaps with the next chapter which digs a little bit deeper into budget, you should have these questions below along with the spreadsheet in the following chapter handy when talking to moving companies.

TIP: Before signing on the dotted line, make sure that the company you end up using for your move is a legitimate company with an excellent record by contacting the BBB/Better Business Bureau. Verify their USDOT number. Do your homework!

QUESTIONS TO ASK

QUESTIONS TO ASK A MOVING TRUCK RENTAL COMPANY

☐ What are your requirements to rent a truck? Age to drive? Can other family members drive the truck?

☐ What is the best way to determine what size truck will I need?

☐ Accepted methods of payment?

☐ Accepted insurance?

☐ How is my quote determined? Any other fees?

☐ Do you offer discounts?

☐ How many miles will I be given for my trip? What if I go over those miles? Fees?

☐ How many days will I be given for my trip? What if I go over? Fees?

☐ What are the fees for renting a hand truck or dolly? Furniture pads?

☐ What do I do if the truck breaks down or has a flat tire?

☐ How many gallons of gas does this truck hold? What is the miles per gallon? Do I return the truck with a full tank of gas?

☐ How far in advance should I reserve a truck? Is the truck guaranteed?

☐ Do you have a cancellation policy?

☐ _____

☐ _____

☐ _____

☐ _____

QUESTIONS TO ASK A FREIGHT/PAY-BY-THE-FOOT COMPANY

☐ Accepted methods of payment?

☐ Accepted insurance?

☐ How are my fees determined? Any other fees?

☐ Do you offer discounts?

☐ What kind of insurance do you provide and what does it cover? How much would it cost to purchase additional coverage?

☐ How many days will it take for the truck to arrive at my destination?

☐ How far in advance should I reserve a truck? Is the truck guaranteed?

☐ Do you have a cancellation policy?

☐ Do you offer storage?

☐ _____

☐ _____

☐ _____

QUESTIONS TO ASK A STORAGE CONTAINER COMPANY

☐ What is the best way to determine what size containers will I need or how many will I need?

☐ How is my quote determined?

☐ Storage fees?

☐ Accepted methods of payment?

☐ Do you offer discounts?

☐ What kind of insurance do you provide and what does it cover? How much would it cost to purchase additional coverage?

☐ How many days will it take for my storage containers to arrive at my destination?

☐ How far in advance should I reserve the storage containers? Are they guaranteed?

☐ Is the delivery of the containers guaranteed?

☐ Do you have a cancellation policy?

☐ _____

☐ _____

☐ _____

QUESTIONS TO ASK A FULL-SERVICE MOVING COMPANY

☐ Is your company licensed? AMSA/American Mover and Storage Association?

☐ What is your USDOT/US Department of Transportation number?

☐ What kind of insurance do you provide and what does it cover? How much would it cost to purchase additional coverage?

☐ How do you determine the weight and cost of moving my belongings?

☐ What methods of payment do you accept?

☐ Do you offer discounts?

☐ Are your employees bonded?

☐ Can I pack my own boxes or does that affect liability?

☐ Will you provide all packing supplies?

☐ Do you guarantee pickup and delivery dates?

☐ How do you handle claims?

☐ Do you offer storage?

☐ What is your cancellation policy?

☐ _____

☐ _____

☐ _____

After contacting a few different companies and asking these questions you may feel confident in what method will work for you and your specific needs. Now let us go to the next chapter where we discuss a moving budget in a bit more detail.

NOTES:

_____

_____

_____

_____

_____

CHAPTER 6: MOVING BUDGET & QUOTES

Your moving budget will likely include more than just getting your belongings from Point A to Point B.

Here are some other things to consider:

Moving supplies: boxes, bubble wrap, etc.

If not using full-service movers you will probably need help moving your heavy pieces of furniture, so make sure that you include the cost of labor. Friends may cost you some pizza and beverages but hired help, either college kids or through local moving companies, will likely cost more. See what the going rates are in your area.

If you are flying to your destination airplane tickets will need to be included.

Flying a pet? They will need a checkup with a veterinarian before the flight, along with the fees for the flight.

If driving, will you be driving your car or a rental? Do not forget to include the cost of gas, tolls, lodging, and meals.

Will you need to make arrangements with an automobile transportation company to deliver your vehicle to your new location? Or will you need to rent a trailer to tow your vehicle behind a truck rental?

So as you can see, your moving budget can extend beyond moving your belongings to your new home. Not only can the price difference between moving methods vary by thousands of dollars, but these other "special circumstances" can also add thousands of dollars to your budget. And that isn't even including fees like deposit, utilities, etc that may be required in your new location.

Moving is a big project and expense so really think about what your needs are and make sure you will be getting what you need for a price that fits your budget. Also it is prudent to add 10% to your personal budget for last minute surprises. You don't want surprises but what is worse than surprises is not being prepared for surprises, so please be prepared.

As soon as you decide, make your reservation with the moving company and the date that works for you.

OK, let's dig deeper into budget.

WAYS TO SAVE MONEY ON YOUR BUDGET

There are a few things that you can do to save money on your moving budget.

Look for free boxes and moving supplies.

Look for coupons and ask for discounts. At the time of this writing I have seen 10% off coupon codes online for various moving companies and have seen where a AAA membership could save you 20% on a Penske truck rental.

Pare down your belongings to the essentials. It will be cheaper to move because you will need fewer packing supplies, smaller truck, fewer storage containers, etc, but don't forget to consider replacement costs.

Summer is peak moving time while kids are out of school, therefore costs are typically higher. If you have the flexibility, moving in Fall, Winter, or Spring could save you money. But if you are moving to or from a location with snow and need to drive through mountain passes for example, that should be a factor to consider.

Also, moving at the end of the month is peak moving time as leases will be expiring so consider moving midmonth if possible. It can also be difficult to find a truck on weekends so if you can move in the middle of the week that too could possibly help.

FORMULATE YOUR BUDGET

MOVING QUOTES   Move Date: _____

COMPANY			
Type of Moving Company (Circle one)	Truck Rental Freight Company Storage Container Full-Service Movers	Truck Rental Freight Company Storage Container Full-Service Movers	Truck Rental Freight Company Storage Container Full-Service Movers
Website			
Phone #			
Contact Person			
Contact Person's Email			
Moving Quote			
Deposit			
Equipment rentals: dollies, furniture pads			
Vehicle Tow Dolly			
Gasoline			
Includes packing supplies?	Y or N	Y or N	Y or N
Includes packing?	Y or N	Y or N	Y or N
Includes loading/ unloading?	Y or N	Y or N	Y or N
Includes labor?	Y or N	Y or N	Y or N
Includes Mileage?	Y or N	Y or N	Y or N
Includes storage?	Y or N	Y or N	Y or N
Storage Unit Fee			
Total of Expenses			

COMPANY			
Type of Moving Company (Circle one)	Truck Rental Freight Company Storage Container Full-Service Movers	Truck Rental Freight Company Storage Container Full-Service Movers	Truck Rental Freight Company Storage Container Full-Service Movers
Website			
Phone #			
Contact Person			
Contact Person's Email			
Moving Quote			
Deposit			
Equipment rentals: dollies, furniture pads			
Vehicle Tow Dolly			
Gasoline			
Includes packing supplies?	Y or N	Y or N	Y or N
Includes packing?	Y or N	Y or N	Y or N
Includes loading/ unloading?	Y or N	Y or N	Y or N
Includes labor?	Y or N	Y or N	Y or N
Includes Mileage?	Y or N	Y or N	Y or N
Includes storage?	Y or N	Y or N	Y or N
Storage Unit Fee			
Total of Expenses			

Now that you have called various moving companies and have received some quotes, it is time to finish building out your budget with the other expenses so that you will have a better idea of what your final expenses will be. Like stated earlier, it is prudent to add 10% to your final budget just in case there are any last minute surprises.

Moving Company Quote	$_____
Car tow dolly	$_____
Taxes	$_____
Additional insurance	$_____
Packing supplies	$_____
Fuel (for moving truck)	$_____
Fuel (for personal vehicle)	$_____
Storage	$_____
Lodging	$_____
Meals	$_____
Tolls	$_____
Airline tickets	$_____
Pet (vet, boarding, and transportation)	$_____
Car shipping	$_____
Tip for movers/labor	$_____
Food and drinks for friends helping	$_____
Deposit and fees for new apartment	$_____
Deposit and fees for utilities	
Electricity	$_____
Gas	$_____
Water	$_____
Cable	$_____
Internet	$_____
Deposit and fees for pet	$_____
_____	$_____
_____	$_____
_____	$_____
_____	$_____
TOTAL	$_____

NOTES:

_____

_____

_____

_____

_____

_____

CHAPTER 7: LEAVING YOUR CURRENT HOME, AND WHAT ABOUT YOUR NEW HOME?

Now let's talk about the last few things that need to be done to leave your current home before heading out to your new home. Do you have the supplies needed to clean your home, or have you hired a service to come in and clean it for you? If you are in a rental, cleaning your home well is usually required to receive your deposit back so make sure you plan ahead to allot the time necessary to do a good job. Are there any last minute repairs that need to be made? Have you pulled out the instruction manuals for the appliances that you will leave behind for the new homeowner if you are selling your house? Warranties? Garage door openers? Keys? Take a few minutes and decide what do you need to do to leave your current home in an inviting state for those who will live there after you leave.

This is also a good time to start planning for your new home. Are there things that you will need to purchase once you get there? If you are a first time home buyer, that may include a lawn mower and other tools for lawn maintenance. If you are going to change the locks, how many locks do you need to change? Have you considered if your furniture will fit in your new home? Where will everything go? (there is graph paper at the end of this book where you can draw out your ideas to scale and decide on furniture placement) It is good to have already thought this through so that as the moving truck is unloaded, things can be put where they belong.

NOTES:

_____

_____

_____

_____

_____

CHAPTER 8: PREPARING FOR YOUR FIRST NIGHT IN YOUR NEW HOME

Congratulations! You are almost home! This is just a friendly reminder to refer to the Moving Timeline on page 34 to make sure everything is still on track and that nothing is forgotten.

Also, this is the perfect time to finalize your box of First Night Essentials, all of those little things that will help make your first night, first morning, and even first couple of days run a little smoother while you begin unpacking and settling into your new home.

FIRST NIGHT ESSENTIALS/MOVE-IN NECESSITIES

This list is an overview of commonly needed items for you first night and day in your new home. This box should be loaded last on the truck rental so that it can be the first off of the truck. Please customize to suit your specific needs.

FOOD & DRINK

☐ coffee/tea

☐ coffee pot/tea kettle

☐ sugar/cream

☐ water, juice, etc

☐ snacks, easy to prepare foods

☐ pot, utensils

☐ napkins

☐ mugs, disposable cups

☐ plates/bowls & silverware

☐ _____

☐ _____

HOUSEHOLD ITEMS

☐ box cutter

☐ scissors

☐ tool kit (screwdriver, wrench, etc)

☐ light bulbs

☐ flashlight

☐ personal devices

☐ chargers for phones and other devices

☐ a couple of dish towels and washcloths

☐ sheets, blankets, and pillows

☐ air mattresses or sleeping bags

☐ shower curtain/rod/rings

☐ _____

PERSONAL CARE

- ☐ toilet paper
- ☐ prescriptions
- ☐ toothbrushes and toothpaste
- ☐ soap, shampoo and conditioner
- ☐ deodorant, lotion
- ☐ hairbrushes and combs
- ☐ towels and washcloths, bath mat
- ☐ suitcases of clothes for everyone
- ☐ diapers for baby
- ☐ toys for your children
- ☐ first aid kit
- ☐ _____

CLEANING SUPPLIES

- ☐ paper towels, cleaning cloths, sponges, etc
- ☐ rubber gloves
- ☐ cleansers
- ☐ dish soap
- ☐ trash bags
- ☐ broom and dustpan, mop
- ☐ vacuum
- ☐ _____
- ☐ _____
- ☐ _____

CHAPTER 9: CHANGE OF ADDRESS

Who to notify when moving goes beyond family and friends, there are also professional organizations, creditors, and more that need to be updated with your new contact information: address, phone number, and sometimes email address. (*Don't forget to update online accounts with address and email changes: newsletters, shopping accounts, etc*).

FINANCIAL

☐ Auto Loans

☐ Banks/Credit Unions

☐ Credit Cards

☐ Employer

☐ Investments

☐ Personal Loans

☐ Student Loans

☐ _____

☐ _____

☐ _____

INSURANCE

☐ Auto

☐ Dental

☐ Health

☐ Homeowner's/Rental

☐ Life

☐ _____

☐ _____

☐ _____

UTILITIES

☐ Cable/Satellite

☐ Electricity

☐ Garbage/Recycling

☐ Gas/Oil

☐ Internet/Cable

☐ Phone

☐ Water

☐ Sewage

☐ _____

☐ _____

☐ _____

HEALTH CARE

☐ Dentists

☐ Doctors

☐ Pharmacy mail order service

☐ Vision

☐ _____

☐ _____

☐ _____

MEMBERSHIPS

☐ Churches

☐ Frequent Flier Programs

☐ Health Clubs

☐ Professional organizations

☐ Magazines/Newspaper

☐ Netflix

☐ Retail Clubs (Costco, Sam's, etc)

☐ Scouts & Youth Organizations

☐ _____

☐ _____

☐ _____

PET CARE

☐ Animal Microchip Registry

☐ Veterinarians

☐ _____

☐ _____

☐ _____

ONLINE SERVICES AND SHOPPING

☐ Amazon

☐ eBay

☐ Paypal

☐ _____

☐ _____

☐ _____

☐ _____

GOVERNMENT

☐ DMV

☐ IRS

☐ Social Security

☐ Voter Registration

☐ Department of Veteran Affairs

☐ Citizenship & Immigration Services

☐ Local/Federal taxes

☐ _____

☐ _____

☐ _____

SOCIAL SECURITY/PENSION

☐ _____

☐ _____

☐ _____

OTHER

☐ Lawyers

☐ Licensing Boards

☐ Babysitter

☐ Cleaning Services

☐ Exterminator

☐ Lawn Care

☐ Snow Removal

☐ _____

☐ _____

☐ _____

FAMILY & FRIENDS

☐ _____   ☐ _____

☐ _____   ☐ _____

☐ _____   ☐ _____

☐ _____   ☐ _____

☐ _____   ☐ _____

☐ _____   ☐ _____

☐ _____   ☐ _____

☐ _____   ☐ _____

☐ _____   ☐ _____

☐ _____   ☐ _____

☐ _____   ☐ _____

☐ _____   ☐ _____

☐ _____   ☐ _____

☐ _____   ☐ _____

☐ _____   ☐ _____

☐ _____   ☐ _____

☐ _____   ☐ _____

☐ _____   ☐ _____

☐ _____   ☐ _____

☐ _____   ☐ _____

CHAPTER 10: MOVING TIMELINE

This timeline is not written in stone, typically it is recommended to start preparing for a move at least 6-8 weeks before the actual move date but I would highly recommend that you start this process as soon as you decide that you will move, even if it is 6-12 months before the move. It just gives you more time to do what needs to be done, like sorting through all of your belongings without a tight time frame looming ahead. Sorting can often be a process that slows people down so make sure that you give yourself enough time to complete the process without being overwhelmed or stressed. Also, by starting the process early enough, you will then be able to begin packing items that you won't be using immediately and begin selling and donating items that you no longer need. Then when you are 1-2 months away from your actual move date you will have a large portion of the process already completed which reduces the stress and enables you to navigate (and even enjoy) the move a bit more.

Here is an example of a typical timeline, please feel free to change it as necessary for your specific needs and add a sticky to the top of this page so that it will be easy to find.

MOVE DATE: _____

2 MONTHS BEFORE MOVE **DATE:** _____

☐ Familiarize yourself with this book so that you know what is in it and where to find it

   ☐ Use a large envelope, folder, pocket, or a binder to keep track of your quotes, paper receipts, etc. If you are going to be reimbursed for this move or can file it on your taxes, this is important.

   ☐ Create a folder on the desktop of your computer for saving digital documents pertinent for your move (quotes, school records, medical records. etc)

☐ Research and collect estimates and quotes from different moving, freight, storage container, and truck rental companies. See pages 24-25 for writing down estimates and quotes. Check reviews and their standing with the Better Business Bureau. Compare their services and prices, then choose one.

   ☐ See page 19 listing questions to ask a truck rental company if choosing that route

   ☐ See pages 19-20 listing questions to ask a freight company if choosing that route

   ☐ See page 20 listing questions to ask a moving container company

   ☐ See page 21 listing questions to ask moving company if choosing that route

☐ After signing, put your contract into your moving folder along with the name, number, and email address of your point of contact, also write your point of contact information into this book in the Contacts section starting on page 50

☐ If your employer is paying for the move, understand their moving policy, allowances, etc

☐ Verify your finalized move date.

☐ Will you need a storage unit at your destination? Get a quote.

☐ If a long distance move, how will you move your vehicles? Drive yourself? Tow it behind a truck rental? Hire an automobile transport company? Get quotes if not driving it yourself.

☐ Finalize budget for the move (See page 26)

☐ If you haven't already, begin researching your new location, community, schools, things to do, etc

☐ Tell your children that you will be moving, make plans to have a going-away party with their friends, make plans to visit their favorite local sites one more time before the move, and introduce them to some of the fun and exciting things that they will be able to experience in their new location. As opportunities arise, engage them in the moving process in an age appropriate way

☐ Collect moving supplies, boxes, tape, etc. See page 6-7 for complete list.

☐ Begin sorting/selling/donating/packing your household belongings

    ☐ If you have plants, see if your mover will move them, many will not due to them being

    so fragile and due to the regulations in some states. Check the laws in your destination state before attempting to move plants across state lines.

    ☐ Create a floor plan and decide if all of your furniture will fit in your new home

    ☐ Set a date for a garage sale

    ☐ Some items sell better through ebay

    ☐ Drop off your donations or have a donation center pick them up

    ☐ Remove batteries from electronics before packing

    ☐ Remove light bulbs from lamps before packing

    ☐ Sort through papers and shred the ones that you no longer need

☐ Begin packing items that you won't be using until after the move such as items in your garage or attic, seasonal decor and books

    ☐ Keep a running inventory of what is in each box on the provided Inventory forms in this book starting on page 59. Make sure each box is numbered (1, 2, 3, etc) and that this number correlations to your inventory sheets. This is important so that when you arrive at your destination you can easily find and then unpack exactly what you need. This inventory is also useful for insurance purpose   35

    ☐ Assign a color to each room and put the appropriate color on the corresponding boxes (for example kitchen orange, living room blue). This allows everyone to know where boxes should be placed when taken off of the truck. You have several options, you can use colored tape, colored dot stickers, or pre-printed colored labels with the names of rooms printed on them.

    ☐ Keep track of serial numbers of important items

    ☐ Take photographs of important items to note condition

    ☐ Valuable items such as jewelry, family heirlooms, photo albums and scrapbooks, baby gear, animal carriers, firearms, and important papers should not be packed, put those aside for you to personally move. Important papers include:

☐ birth certificates	☐ school records
☐ marriage license	☐ pet records
☐ other licenses	☐ prescriptions
☐ Social Security cards	☐ financial records
☐ passports	☐ insurance policies
☐ vehicle titles	☐ power of attorney
☐ wills	☐ _____
☐ stocks	☐ _____
☐ medical records	

☐ Call your insurance companies and see if you need to make any changes to your policy:

☐ auto	☐ house
☐ medical	☐ life

☐ Go through your home room-by-room and assess what needs to be done

    ☐ repairs

    ☐ painting

    ☐ carpet cleaning

    ☐ thorough, deep cleaning

    ☐ _____

    ☐ _____

    ☐ _____

☐ If you are selling your home, hire a real estate agent, or if renting, notify your landlord of your move-out-date.

☐ Give notice to your employer, update your resume and begin looking for a new job if needed

☐ Start using up items that you don't want to move: frozen and perishable foods, canned goods, cleaning supplies, etc

☐ _____

☐ _____

☐ _____

6 WEEKS BEFORE MOVE   DATE: _____

☐ Continue to add any new contracts, forms, and receipts to binder and folder

☐ Decide on needs for a new home (rental or purchase) and finalize

☐ Make travel arrangements: plane tickets and a car rental if needed, or if driving, plan out your trip, stops, hotels, any interesting sites to see along the way, etc.

☐ If moving a pet, decide if your pet will fly or ride in the car. Discuss this with your veterinarian, decide if you need medication to relax your pet

    ☐ if driving, make sure that you make reservations for hotels that accept pets in advance

    ☐ also, don't forget to pack pet food and bowls for food and water for the road trip, litter box or bags for bathroom breaks, blankets/toys, leashes, and collars with tags

☐ Contact your children's schools and have records transferred to new school

☐ Schedule appointments before the move: dental, medical, and vision and get new prescriptions

☐ See if you need to refill any prescriptions so that you don't run out during the move

☐ Get copies of medical and dental records or have them transferred

☐ Schedule last appointments and grooming for your pets if needed

☐ Get copies of pet medical records

☐ Fill out change of address form from the post office

☐ If you think you may not remember how to put furniture pieces back together, take photographs before you take it apart. Take a zippered food storage bag and with a permanent marker label the bag with the name of the furniture piece (example: Susie's desk), then put the screws, nuts, and bolts into the bag. You can tape the bag to the underside or back of the furniture boards, or keep all of the zippered bags together in a box with your tools

☐ Continue packing

☐ _____

☐ _____

☐ _____

4 WEEKS BEFORE MOVE   DATE: _____

☐ Continue to add any new contracts, forms, and receipts to binder and folder

☐ Take your vehicle in for a check-up before the move (brakes, fluid levels, alignment, tires, etc)

☐ Pack a box of essentials to have the first night in your new home (See page 29-30 for a list of First Night Essentials)

☐ If you need help loading a truck rental, ask friends to help on moving day

☐ Photograph valuable belongings and have them appraised

☐ Arrange for these services to be disconnected the day after you move:

☐ electricity	☐ cable/satellite
☐ gas	☐ trash/recycling
☐ water	☐ home security system
☐ telephone	☐ _____
☐ internet	☐ _____

☐ Schedule vacation time for move if necessary

☐ Open a bank account in your new location unless your bank already has a branch there

☐ Return library books or anything borrowed or rented

☐ Retrieve items loaned out to others

☐ Cancel automated electronic payments if necessary

☐ Cancel local memberships if necessary

    ☐ gym

    ☐ _____

    ☐ _____

☐ Have things handy to occupy your children: toys, books, crayons and paper, etc

☐ Familiarize yourself with hazardous items that are not allowed to be loaded and transported. Make plans to use up these items if possible or give them away (See page 10-11 for a list, but also contact your mover to get their updated list)

☐ Schedule to have a cleaning company clean your new home right before your move-in date

☐ Continue packing

☐ _____

☐ _____

☐ _____

2 WEEKS BEFORE MOVE   DATE: _____

☐ Continue to add any new contracts, forms, and receipts to binder and folder

☐ Confirm moving arrangements with moving company/truck rental facility

☐ Arrange to have help available to unload truck if necessary

☐ Will you need a permit at your new home for the moving truck? Get a permit if necessary.

☐ Arrange to have your utilities turned on at your new home one day before you arrive

    ☐ electricity   ☐ cable/satellite

    ☐ gas   ☐ trash/recycling

    ☐ water   ☐ _____

    ☐ telephone   ☐ _____

    ☐ internet

☐ Last chance to refill any needed prescriptions

☐ Provide your new address to:

    ☐ Family   ☐ Automobile loans

    ☐ Friends   ☐ Cell phone company

    ☐ Employer   ☐ Monthly memberships such as Netflix

    ☐ Schools

    ☐ Attorney, accountant, financial planner, etc   ☐ Insurance policies: medical, dental, life, auto, etc

    ☐ Social Security/pension   ☐ Employer

    ☐ Investment accounts like 401k and IRA accounts   ☐ Personal loans

    ☐ Pharmacy mail service   ☐ Professional organizations and journals

    ☐ Magazine and newspaper subscriptions   ☐ Online accounts like eBay, Paypal, and Amazon

    ☐ Bank accounts   ☐ _____

    ☐ Credit cards   ☐ _____

                              ☐ _____

☐ If you have a safety deposit box, empty the contents and put them with the valuables that you will personally move

☐ Call your credit card companies and let them know of your move so that you will be able to use your credit cards on the road

☐ If you have drapes, have them cleaned before packing. Make sure that you have picked up everything from the dry cleaners

☐ Have your rugs and carpets cleaned

☐ Make arrangements for childcare for the day of the move

☐ If your pet will be flying, obtain a health certificate from your veterinarian dated within 10 days of flight

☐ Continue packing

☐ Have vehicle maintenance check before move (tires, alignment, brakes, fluid levels, etc)

☐ _____

☐ _____

☐ _____

1 WEEK BEFORE MOVE   DATE: _____

☐ Confirm moving arrangements with moving company/truck rental facility

☐ Make sure your First Night Essentials boxes/baskets are put to the side and labeled, or even put in a closet out of the way so that they are loaded into the truck last and unloaded first (you do not want them to be in the back of the moving truck).

☐ Check that you have collected your valuable items and put them in a box for you to personally move, as noted in the first section, 2 Months Before Move. Label the box "Do Not Pack" and put it aside so that it is not packed.

☐ Get a small box and put in items that will go to the people moving in: keys, garage door opener, manuals for appliances that are staying, etc. Also leave them your new address so that they can forward any stray mail.

☐ Make sure your car kit is complete

      ☐ jumper cables

      ☐ water and snacks

      ☐ first aid kit

      ☐ flashlight (crank or have extra batteries on hand)

      ☐ radio (crank or have extra batteries on hand)

      ☐ car cell phone charger

      ☐ gloves

      ☐ blanket

☐ toilet paper and baby wipes

☐ shovel

☐ if moving when there is a chance of snow, make sure that you update your car kit to include winter items such as an ice scraper, kitty litter and chains for your tires

☐ _____

☐ _____

☐ _____

☐ _____

☐ If hiring movers, make sure that you know what type of payment is acceptable (credit card, check, cash, money order, etc) and have cash for a tip.

☐ Make plans to pick up the truck rental if using one

☐ Prepare a Moving Day box

    ☐ Buy drinks and snacks for movers or friends helping you move

    ☐ have toilet paper available, and soap and paper towels for washing hands

    ☐ trash bags

    ☐ tape, tape dispenser, markers

    ☐ first aid kit

☐ Prepare a basket/box for the rental truck and your vehicle if driving it yourself, include maps, drinks and snacks, toys and games for your children, devices and their chargers, blankets and pillows, prescriptions, important papers pertinent to your move, etc. If you are driving with your pet, bring pet food, water, bowls, bedding, and bags for bathroom breaks

☐ Make sure the place is ready for you to move out

    ☐ nail holes caulked and painted

    ☐ a couple of days before the move clean your house thoroughly or hire a cleaner

    ☐ clean bathrooms, kitchen, windows, stove/oven, refrigerator, etc

    ☐ make sure the lawn is mowed, bushes trimmed, etc

☐ Drain the gas and oil from power equipment (lawn mower, edger, chainsaw, etc)

☐ Prepare the appliances that you will be moving:

    ☐ for the refrigerator, make sure the freezer is defrosted, empty the ice cube trays and ice maker, drain the water from hose, and leave doors open so that it can dry thoroughly

☐ after doing your last load of laundry, prepare the washing machine and dryer for the move, such as drain water from washing machine hose and leave the door open so that it can dry out

☐ _____

☐ _____

☐ _____

☐ Start packing suitcases of clothes and toiletries for your trip

☐ Any non-perishable food items that you won't be able to eat or don't want to move can be donated to a local food pantry

☐ Make a last run to drop off donations or schedule for a pickup

☐ Return cable box and remote

☐ Back up computer files

☐ Movers will not move hazardous materials, last chance to remove any and all hazardous materials

☐ Cancel services that you won't be utilizing at new address (or if moving locally, provide new address):

    ☐ lawn care

    ☐ cleaning service

    ☐ newspaper

    ☐ pool

    ☐ water delivery

☐ Remove satellite, portable air conditioners, outdoor play equipment, sheds, garden art, birdfeeders, etc. Clean if packing, donate or sell if not keeping.

☐ Clean any outdoor furniture that is going with you on the move. Donate or sell that you are not keeping.

☐ Drain water from garden hoses

☐ _____

☐ _____

1 DAY BEFORE MOVE   DATE: _____

☐ Make sure diaper bag is topped off with diapers, wipes, clothes, blankets, etc for baby

☐ Make sure your suitcases are packed and put to the side so that they are not loaded into the back of the moving truck

☐ Unplug electronics and appliances so that they can cool off for the move

☐ Make sure your First Night Essentials boxes/baskets are put to the side so that they are loaded last (you do not want them to be in the back of the moving truck), or put them in the trunk of your car.

☐ _____

☐ _____

MOVING DAY - LOADING   DATE: _____

☐ Before the moving truck arrives, put your box of valuables in the trunk of your car

☐ Put your suitcases in the trunk of your car

☐ Pick up truck rental if using one

☐ Wear comfortable clothes and shoes

☐ Young children need to be watched by the babysitter

☐ Pets need to be boarded or watched by the pet sitter

☐ Remove bedding from beds, take beds apart

☐ Begin loading the truck, loading heavy items first (such as furniture and large appliances), and fill in tightly, working your way to the end of the truck with boxes and everything else

☐ Go through your house one more time

    ☐ make sure everything is packed and loaded

    ☐ house is clean

    ☐ make sure all windows are locked

    ☐ vacuum your way out of the home, start in the back, work your way to the door, turning off lights along the way

    ☐ doors are locked

    ☐ trash is thrown away

☐ Load these items last in the truck rental so that they are available first for unloading

    ☐ First Night Essentials boxes

    ☐ forearm strap

    ☐ hand truck

    ☐ box cutter/utility knife

☐ Lock up truck rental with padlock

☐ Give your keys to real estate agent or landlord

☐ Add your moving binder and this book to your box of valuables

☐ _____

☐ _____

☐ _____

MOVING DAY - UNLOADING   **DATE:** _____

☐ Have funds (credit card, cashier's check, etc) ready for the final payment upon delivery of your goods

☐ Have the necessary supplies for unloading the truck available:

    ☐ forearm strap   ☐ trash bags

    ☐ hand truck

45

☐ Post the color assigned for each room on their doorways so that boxes can be put in the correct room

☐ As boxes and items are unloaded, check them off of inventory list

☐ Check boxes and items for damage, take photos before signing the release/bill of lading from the movers. If damage is found on boxes not yet unpacked, leave the boxes untouched and call the moving company. Know the deadline to report insurance claims.

☐ Make sure that all of your utilities are on and everything is functioning

      ☐ water

      ☐ gas

      ☐ electricity

      ☐ heat/air conditioning

      ☐ phone

      ☐ water heater

      ☐ toilets

☐ Make sure that furniture is assembled correctly

☐ Have your heavy furniture put into position based on your layout while you have the help

☐ Unpack in order of importance and immediate use, like your First Night Essentials box, beds, linens, and kitchen (use your inventory list)

☐ Child-proof anything that needs it

☐ Help your pet get accustomed to their new home

☐ Make a grocery store run for perishables (milk, eggs, juice, etc)

☐ Change the locks on your new home

☐ Make sure that all windows are locked

☐ _____

☐ _____

☐ _____

WEEK AFTER MOVING DAY

DATE: _____

☐ Update your driver's license, license plate, and registration

☐ Register to vote

☐ Make sure that fire alarms are in working order

☐ After settled in, update home inventory

☐ Take photographs of your belongings in your new home for insurance purposes

☐ Update home or rental insurance if necessary

☐ Find a new doctor, dentist, pharmacy, veterinarian, etc

☐ Send thank you cards to those who helped during the move

☐ Check to see when you will receive your rental or moving deposits back if applicable

☐ Donate your boxes or recycle

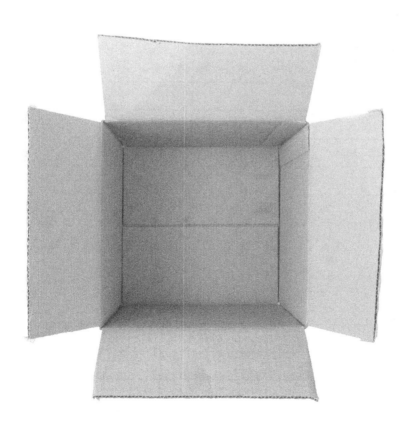

COMMAND CENTER

IMPORTANT INFORMATION AT YOUR FINGERTIPS

Move Date: _____ Arrival Date: _____

Our Contact Information

Old Address: _____

_____

New Address: _____

_____

Phone #1: _____

Phone #2: _____

Email: _____

Mover's Contact Information

Company: _____

Contact: _____

Phone: _____

Email: _____

Start Mileage: _____ | End Mileage: _____

Total Miles: _____

Fuel type: _____

NOTES

_____

_____

_____

_____

COMMAND CENTER

TRIP DETAILS

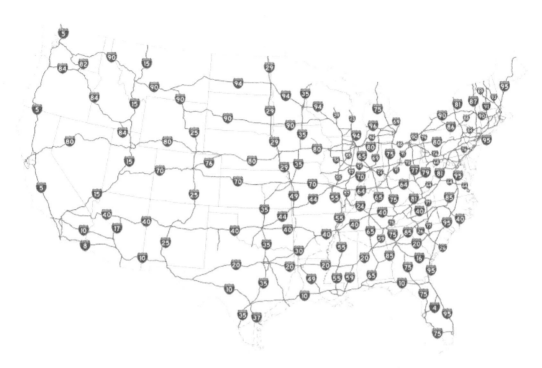

(Use this map or paste a print-out of your trip here)

Mark your internary, hotel stops, etc

Day	DESTINATION	MILES START END	HOTEL	NOTES
DAY 1		-		
DAY 2		-		
DAY 3		-		
DAY 4		-		
DAY 5		-		

CONTACTS

COMPANY _____

Website _____

Account # _____

Password _____

Phone _____

Contact _____

Email _____

Notes _____

_____

_____

COMPANY _____

Website _____

Account # _____

Password _____

Phone _____

Contact _____

Email _____

Notes _____

_____

_____

COMPANY _____

Website _____

Account # _____

Password _____

Phone _____

Contact _____

Email _____

Notes _____

_____

_____

CONTACTS

COMPANY _____

Website _____

Account # _____

Password _____

Phone _____

Contact _____

Email _____

Notes _____

_____

_____

_____

COMPANY _____

Website _____

Account # _____

Password _____

Phone _____

Contact _____

Email _____

Notes _____

_____

_____

COMPANY _____

Website _____

Account # _____

Password _____

Phone _____

Contact _____

Email _____

Notes _____

_____

_____

_____

CONTACTS

COMPANY
_____

Website
_____

Account #
_____

Password
_____

Phone
_____

Contact
_____

Email
_____

Notes
_____

_____

_____

COMPANY
_____

Website
_____

Account #
_____

Password
_____

Phone
_____

Contact
_____

Email
_____

Notes
_____

_____

_____

COMPANY
_____

Website
_____

Account #
_____

Password
_____

Phone
_____

Contact
_____

Email
_____

Notes
_____

_____

_____

CONTACTS

COMPANY _____

Website _____

Account # _____

Password _____

Phone _____

Contact _____

Email _____

Notes _____

_____

_____

_____

COMPANY _____

Website _____

Account # _____

Password _____

Phone _____

Contact _____

Email _____

Notes _____

_____

_____

COMPANY _____

Website _____

Account # _____

Password _____

Phone _____

Contact _____

Email _____

Notes _____

_____

_____

CONTACTS

COMPANY

Website _____

Account # _____

Password _____

Phone _____

Contact _____

Email _____

Notes _____

_____

_____

COMPANY

Website _____

Account # _____

Password _____

Phone _____

Contact _____

Email _____

Notes _____

_____

_____

COMPANY

Website _____

Account # _____

Password _____

Phone _____

Contact _____

Email _____

Notes _____

_____

_____

CONTACTS

COMPANY _____

Website _____

Account # _____

Password _____

Phone _____

Contact _____

Email _____

Notes _____

_____

_____

_____

COMPANY _____

Website _____

Account # _____

Password _____

Phone _____

Contact _____

Email _____

Notes _____

_____

_____

COMPANY _____

Website _____

Account # _____

Password _____

Phone _____

Contact _____

Email _____

Notes _____

_____

_____

_____

CONTACTS

COMPANY

Website

Account #

Password

Phone

Contact

Email

Notes

COMPANY

Website

Account #

Password

Phone

Contact

Email

Notes

COMPANY

Website

Account #

Password

Phone

Contact

Email

Notes

CONTACTS

COMPANY _____

Website _____

Account # _____

Password _____

Phone _____

Contact _____

Email _____

Notes _____

_____

_____

_____

COMPANY _____

Website _____

Account # _____

Password _____

Phone _____

Contact _____

Email _____

Notes _____

_____

_____

COMPANY _____

Website _____

Account # _____

Password _____

Phone _____

Contact _____

Email _____

Notes _____

_____

_____

CONTACTS

COMPANY _____

Website _____

Account # _____

Password _____

Phone _____

Contact _____

Email _____

Notes _____

_____

_____

_____

COMPANY _____

Website _____

Account # _____

Password _____

Phone _____

Contact _____

Email _____

Notes _____

_____

_____

_____

COMPANY _____

Website _____

Account # _____

Password _____

Phone _____

Contact _____

Email _____

Notes _____

_____

_____

_____

INVENTORY

ROOM: COLOR:

BOX #	CONTENTS	LOADED	ARRIVED

INVENTORY

ROOM: COLOR:

BOX #	CONTENTS	LOADED	ARRIVED

INVENTORY

ROOM: COLOR:

BOX #	CONTENTS	LOADED	ARRIVED

INVENTORY

ROOM: COLOR:

BOX #	CONTENTS	LOADED	ARRIVED

INVENTORY

ROOM: COLOR:

BOX #	CONTENTS	LOADED	ARRIVED

INVENTORY

ROOM: COLOR:

BOX #	CONTENTS	LOADED	ARRIVED

INVENTORY

ROOM: COLOR:

BOX #	CONTENTS	LOADED	ARRIVED

INVENTORY

ROOM: COLOR:

BOX #	CONTENTS	LOADED	ARRIVED

INVENTORY

ROOM: COLOR:

BOX #	CONTENTS	LOADED	ARRIVED

INVENTORY

ROOM: _____   COLOR: _____

BOX #	CONTENTS	LOADED	ARRIVED

INVENTORY

ROOM: COLOR:

BOX #	CONTENTS	LOADED	ARRIVED

69

INVENTORY

ROOM: COLOR:

BOX #	CONTENTS	LOADED	ARRIVED

INVENTORY

ROOM: COLOR:

BOX #	CONTENTS	LOADED	ARRIVED

INVENTORY

ROOM: COLOR:

BOX #	CONTENTS	LOADED	ARRIVED

INVENTORY

ROOM: COLOR:

BOX #	CONTENTS	LOADED	ARRIVED

INVENTORY

ROOM: COLOR:

BOX #	CONTENTS	LOADED	ARRIVED

INVENTORY

ROOM: COLOR:

BOX #	CONTENTS	LOADED	ARRIVED

INVENTORY

ROOM: COLOR:

BOX #	CONTENTS	LOADED	ARRIVED

INVENTORY

ROOM: COLOR:

BOX #	CONTENTS	LOADED	ARRIVED

INVENTORY

ROOM: COLOR:

BOX #	CONTENTS	LOADED	ARRIVED

INVENTORY

ROOM: COLOR:

BOX #	CONTENTS	LOADED	ARRIVED

INVENTORY

ROOM: COLOR:

BOX #	CONTENTS	LOADED	ARRIVED

INVENTORY

ROOM: COLOR:

BOX #	CONTENTS	LOADED	ARRIVED

INVENTORY

ROOM: COLOR:

BOX #	CONTENTS	LOADED	ARRIVED

INVENTORY

ROOM: COLOR:

BOX #	CONTENTS	LOADED	ARRIVED

INVENTORY

ROOM: COLOR:

BOX #	CONTENTS	LOADED	ARRIVED

84

INVENTORY

ROOM: _____ COLOR: _____

BOX #	CONTENTS	LOADED	ARRIVED

INVENTORY

ROOM: COLOR:

BOX #	CONTENTS	LOADED	ARRIVED

INVENTORY

ROOM: _____   COLOR: _____

BOX #	CONTENTS	LOADED	ARRIVED

INVENTORY

ROOM: COLOR:

BOX #	CONTENTS	LOADED	ARRIVED

INVENTORY

ROOM: COLOR:

BOX #	CONTENTS	LOADED	ARRIVED

INVENTORY

ROOM: COLOR:

BOX #	CONTENTS	LOADED	ARRIVED

INVENTORY

ROOM: COLOR:

BOX #	CONTENTS	LOADED	ARRIVED

INVENTORY

ROOM: COLOR:

BOX #	CONTENTS	LOADED	ARRIVED

(Grid paper for notes, layout and placement of furniture in new home, etc)

(Grid paper for notes, layout and placement of furniture in new home, etc)

(Grid paper for notes, layout and placement of furniture in new home, etc)

(Grid paper for notes, layout and placement of furniture in new home, etc)

(Grid paper for notes, layout and placement of furniture in new home, etc)

(Grid paper for notes, layout and placement of furniture in new home, etc)

Made in the USA
Monee, IL
16 May 2024

58533022R00057